Celebrating you

1971

a very special year for

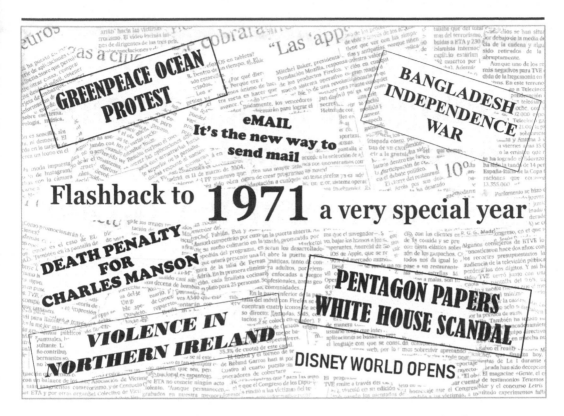

Flashback to **1971** a very special year

GREENPEACE OCEAN PROTEST

BANGLADESH INDEPENDENCE WAR

eMAIL It's the new way to send mail

DEATH PENALTY FOR CHARLES MANSON

PENTAGON PAPERS WHITE HOUSE SCANDAL

VIOLENCE IN NORTHERN IRELAND

DISNEY WORLD OPENS

Let's flashback to 1971, a very special year.

Was this the year you were born?

Was this the year you were married?

Whatever the reason, this book is a celebration of your year,

THE YEAR 1971.

Turn the pages to discover a book packed with fun-filled fabulous facts. We look at the people, the places, the politics and the pleasures that made 1971 unique and helped shape the world we know today.

So get your time-travel suit on, and enjoy this trip down memory lane, to rediscover what life was like, back in the year 1971.

Instead of giving your teenager another sermon on sloppy handwriting, give him a Smith-Corona.

He's probably heard enough sermons to recite them by heart.

And has it done any good?

If not, perhaps it's time you tried something else.

Perhaps it's time for a Smith-Corona? Like our electric portable.

With it, your teenager can learn to type twice as fast as writing by hand.

His spelling can improve because a typed word that's misspelled just begs to be corrected.

Thinking gets a nudge, too, because a typewriter can accept ideas as fast as they appear.

And then a quiet little miracle called Organization occurs. When that happens, pride, confidence and self-esteem can start to show themselves.

It's smooth sailing from there.

But why Smith-Corona?

Because all typewriters are not the same.

That's why we invite you to <u>compare a</u> Smith-Corona against any other typewriter.

<u>Compare</u> durability. Portability. Features.

<u>Compare</u> years of experience in manufacturing (especially electric portables).

When you do, you'll know why more people in the world buy Smith-Corona Electric Portables than any other.

And why you should, too.

You'll find our dealers in the Yellow Pages. **SCM**.

SMITH-CORONA

**We think we make better students.
We know we make better typewriters.**

He's probably heard enough sermons to recite them by heart. And has it done any good? If not, perhaps it's time you tried something else. Perhaps it's time for a Smith-Corona. Like our electric portable. With it, your teenager can learn to type twice as fast as writing by hand. His spelling can improve because a typed word that's misspelled just begs to be corrected. Thinking gets a nudge, too, because a typewriter can accept ideas as fast as they appear. And then a quiet little miracle called Organization occurs. When that happens, pride, confidence and self-esteem can start to show themselves. It's smooth sailing from there.

But why Smith-Corona?

Because all typewriters are not the same. That's why we invite you to compare a Smith-Corona against any other typewriter. Compare durability. Portability. Features. Compare years of experience in manufacturing (especially electric portables).

When you do, you'll know why more people in the world buy Smith-Corona Electric Portables than any other. And why you should, too. You'll find our dealers in the Yellow Pages.

Contents

1971 Family Life in the USA

Imagine if time-travel was a reality, and one fine morning you wake up to find yourself flashed back in time, back to the year 1971.

What would life be like for a typical family, in a typical town, somewhere in America?

Young people at a May Day concert, 1st May 1971.

In the early 70s our cultural gaze had shifted away from London's Swinging Sixties, back to the USA. The hippie view of the world, with its emphasis on peace, love and nature, focused our collective attention on the anti-war and anti-pollution movements.

We were fed-up with the ongoing Cold War and the draining war in Vietnam. We were ready for a new focus and a new vision. The counterculture movements of the late 60s continued well into the 1970s, as we rejected the old traditions and conservative values of our parents. Women, African Americans, LGBT communities and environmentalists would ramp up the fight for recognition and equality.

In the ten years to 1971, the US population had increased by 11.5% to 211.4 million.[1] The first of the Baby Boomers were now a vocal population of young adults. Birth rates and family sizes were falling, thanks to changing family values and readily available contraceptives.

May Day protest, Washington D.C. 1971.
Women's Strike for Equality march, 26th Aug 1970, New York, USA.

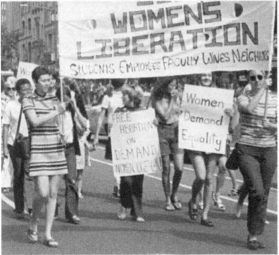

At the same time, divorce rates were rising. The feminist movement had left women more educated and confident. As no-fault divorce laws came into effect, couples could legally divorce for any or no reason at all. An estimated 50% of couples who married in 1971 would end up divorced in future years.[2]

Levels of education had also increased–80% of 17-year-olds graduated high school in 1971 (up from 69.5% ten years earlier).[3] A further 36% of 18 to 19-year-olds continued to a higher education institution.

[1] worldometers.info/world-population.
[2] nationalaffairs.com/publications/detail/the-evolution-of-divorce.
[3] usafacts.org/data/topics/people-society/education.
[4] statista.com/statistics/236093/higher-education-enrollment-rates-by-age-group-us.

The picture is brighter in America's parking lots.

Driving up to a Fotomat® store is just about the easiest way in the whole world to get a roll of pictures developed.

Plus your pictures themselves will probably look better.

We're the country's largest retailer of photographic services. With over 1,000 drive-through stores in parking lots coast-to-coast. With a few exceptions.

Such as the Fotomat store that opened with "SIX FLAGS OVER MID-AMERICA" this summer in St. Louis. It's a living history book built over 200 magnificently landscaped acres. There are rides like the famous Log Flume, and shows for everyone in the family—and we're inside the gates.

We want to make picture-taking easier. Anywhere we are.

Driving up to a Fotomat store is just about the easiest way in the whole world to get a roll of pictures developed.

Plus your pictures themselves will probably look better.

We're the country's largest retailer of photographic services. With over 1,000 drive-through stores in parking lots coast-to-coast. With a few exceptions.

Such as the Fotomat store that opened with "six flags over mid-America" this summer in St. Louis. It's a living history book built over 200 magnificently landscaped acres. There are rides like the famous Log Flume, and shows for everyone in the family—and we're inside the gates.

We want to make picture-taking easier. Anywhere we are.

Did you know that the term "generation gap" was coined by the Baby Boomers to describe the differences between their attitudes and values, and those of their old-world parents? This new generation questioned everything about "the American Dream", even mixing their social and political views into their music and art.

A family portrait, 1970.

Universities and colleges became breeding grounds for free-thinking, liberal theories. Students often shared accommodation, partly for convenience and cost savings, but also as an expression of a new way of living, cohabiting, exploring sexual freedoms and spiritual fulfilment.

College students on campus, 1971.

In 1971 the median family income was $10,290 a year, unemployment stood at 6%, with GDP at 3.3%.[1]

Average costs in 1971 [2]	
New house	$25,250
New car	$3,500
Dishwasher	$180
A gallon of gasoline	$0.36

[1] census.gov/library/publications.html, and thebalance.com/unemployment-rate-by-year-3305506.
[2] thepeoplehistory.com and mclib.info/reference/local-history-genealogy/historic-prices/.

Life in the United Kingdom

Now just imagine you flashed back to a town in 1971 England. Although not all doom and gloom, the United Kingdom had found itself slipping on the world stage as America and the USSR battled for domination.

London had reigned as the center of global culture during the decade of the 60s, but by the 70s the shine had mostly faded. The joyful, care-free optimism of England's Swinging Sixties could not last forever.

London street scenes from the early 70s.

The sentiment on the streets had shifted from frivolity to revolution. This attitude was echoed in the fashion, music, art and culture of the time.

The "Troubles" in Northern Ireland affected the mood of the Nation. Nationalist campaigns had become increasingly violent, spilling into the streets of cities across the UK as activists took to bombing commercial and political targets.

The British feminist movement had a long established history and continued to gain strength throughout the 1970s.

In March 1971, 4,000 women took to the streets for the first march of the newly formed Women's Liberation Movement. Their list of equal rights demands included equal education, equal pay, and free contraception.

The first Women's Liberation Movement protest march, 8th March 1971.

In 1971 the average age of marriage for women was 25, and the average age for the birth of their first child was 27.[1] The fertility rate was 2.2 births per woman, down from a peak of 2.9 in 1964.[2] The contraceptive pill (available since 1961) and the legalisation of abortion in 1967 aided in this decline.

The Divorce Reform Act came into effect in January 1971, allowing for divorce without reason and leading to a steep increase in divorce rates.

In the early 70s less than 50% of families owned a car.[3] Within the larger cities, most people still relied on public transport.

10% of homes did not have internal toilets, while 9% were still without baths. 58% lacked telephones and 66% lacked central heating.[4]

Only 33% of 18-year-olds finished high school, a figure far lower than most other industrialized nations.

[1&2] ons.gov.uk/peoplepopulationandcommunity.
[3] racfoundation.org/wp-content/uploads/2017/11/car-ownership.
[4] bbc.com/news/magazine-21698533.

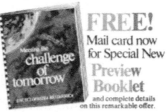
You get all volumes now... pay later on easy Book a Month Payment Plan.

Yes, the latest edition of Britannica–the greatest treasury of knowledge ever published–is now available on a remarkable Cooperative Offer. Under the terms of this amazing offer, you may obtain the latest edition of Britannica Junior *at no extra cost* when you choose Encyclopaedia Britannica. Also included, *free*, the Britannica Pre-School Library–*First Adventures in Learning*. The 3 complete sets will be placed in your home NOW. You pay *later* on convenient budget terms. *Easy as buying a book a month.*

The Britannica Pre-School Library–*First Adventures in Learning*–is now available from Britannica. It represents years of editorial and educational experience and was designed to provide every child with better pre-school preparation. This Pre-School Library offers a wealth of exciting new materials which acquaint the smaller child with the world in which he lives through simple words, pictures, and signs.

Britannica Junior is a big, 15-volume set written, illustrated, and indexed especially for children in grade school and junior high. Carefully matched to school subjects as a homework reference, it's rich in picture interest, and is easy to read and understand. And it leads right into encyclopaedia Britannica.

Encyclopaedia Britannica Offers Thousands of Subjects of Practical Value. The new edition of Britannica has special articles on household budgets, interior decorating, medicine, health, home remodeling, child care and much more... useful information that can save you many dollars.

Essential for Homework. For students, Britannica is indispensable. It is the finest, most complete reference published in America. It helps develop the active, alert minds that bring success in school and later life.

At midnight on 15th February 1971, after years of planning, the UK switched to the new decimal currency.

Decimal Conversion Rates	
SHILLINGS	1/- = 5p
	5/- = 25p
	10/- = 50p
	12/- = 60p
	19/- = 95p
PENNIES	1d = ½p
	2d = 1p
	3d = 1p
	4d = 1½p
	5d = 2p
	6d = 2½p

Posters for the new decimal system were displayed everywhere.

By 1971 the UK was nearly half-way through repaying its post-war debt to America and Canada. The 20-year post-war building boom, which had kept cash flowing and unemployment low, was over.

Economic growth in the UK was only half that of Germany and Japan, with annual GDP having slipped from 2nd place in 1960 (behind only USA), to 5th place in 1971. Moreover, UK GDP per capita had slipped to 24th place in world rankings.[1]

Industrial Relations Bill protest, 1st March 1971.

By 1971, most of the former colonies of the United Kingdom had been granted independence. The cost for the UK to keep and defend them had proven too high a burden.

Industrial strife was high, and inflation was on the rise. The UK in 1971 was a country in decline. And this was just the beginning. The worse was yet to come.

The remainder of the decade would bring a mounting series of economic crises, industrial actions and major political battles.

Engineering workers' strike at Tower Hill, London, 1st March 1973.

[1] nationmaster.com/country-info/stats/Economy/GDP.

Hippies and the Rise of the Communes

By the early 70s, the Baby Boomers were young adults. Everything about them was a break-away from their parents: their music, their fashion, their values, their personal and sexual freedoms. They were non-traditional, non-conformists, anti-war, anti-authority, politically active, experimental drug users, hippies, believers and disbelievers. Anything was possible. Everything was acceptable.

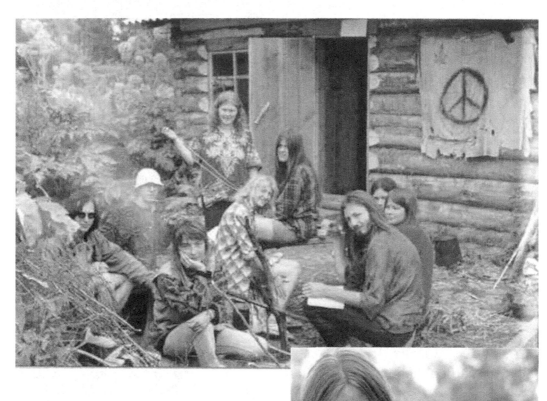

The rise of communal living in the late 60s and early 70s was yet another expression of freedom of choice. Communes were an experiment, communes were anti-establishment, communes were whatever the inhabitants chose them to be.

Most communes encouraged co-ownership of possessions, collective chores and shared child-raising. For many, clothes, monogamy and drug usage were optional. By rejecting the 40-hour work week, many communards relied on food stamps, or temporary odd-jobs to keep themselves nourished.

In rural areas communards practiced living off the land, setting up farms, building their own houses and selling handicrafts.

Myrtle Hill Farm, Vermont.

A geodesic dome house built at Myrtle Hill Farm, Vermont. Recalls one communard, "In 1971 a young man named Bernie Sanders visited Myrtle Hill Farm... Sanders' tendency to just sit around talking politics and avoid actual physical labor got him the boot."[1]

Communards at Hog Farm, California.

The rise of communal living in the late 60s and early 70s was worldwide. Although the vast majority only survived a few years, some communes continue to exist today.

[1] From *We Are As Gods: Back to the Land in the 1970s on the Quest for a New America* by Brian Doherty.

We want to introduce as many people as possible to the finest-designed, best-built Chryslers we've ever offered. So we're coming through with the Royal. A brand-new series of Chryslers. At a new low price. $112 less than any other Chrysler series.

Royal is every inch a Chrysler. Uncompromisingly full-sized.

Royal is just as big as our most expensive New Yorker.

It's also a bigger car than our chief competition, Buick LeSabre and Olds Delta 88.

With a roomier interior. And a bigger trunk.

Even the engine is bigger.

Royal also comes with a torsion-bar suspension system. LeSabre and Delta use coil springs. Which is better?

Well, it's interesting to note that GM does use torsion bars on two models; one of the most expensive Cadillacs, and the most expensive Oldsmobile.

Now are we coming through?

Royal. An introduction to what a full-sized car should be.

A Chrysler. At a price you can afford.

Our Love Affair with Automobiles

Our love affair with automobiles began back in the early 50s, and by 1971 America's car addiction was unrivalled in the world. More than 92 million vehicles traveled our roads. Vehicle numbers had risen 50% during the preceding 10 years. Although automobile costs had risen markedly, so too had real wages, making cars increasingly affordable. The family car had become a necessity we could not survive without.

Americans purchased 10,155,000 cars in 1971, setting a new record.

Increased car ownership and the creation of the National Highway System gave us a new sense of freedom. Office commuters could live further out from city centers, in cleaner and more spacious suburban developments, and commute quickly and comfortably to work.

Traffic congestion in Boston, 1971.

Rural areas faced a steady decline as the suburban population continued to rise. By the early 1970s, only 26% of the population remained in rural areas.

SouthPark Mall in Charlotte, North Carolina, 1971.

Catering to the suburban lifestyle, fully enclosed, air-conditioned shopping malls sprang up country-wide. A typical design saw one or two anchor stores with hundreds of smaller specialty shops sitting within a vast expanse of carparks.

DEMON 340
...the performance is a lot more than painted on.

Detroit was the car manufacturing powerhouse of America, where "the Big Three" (Ford, General Motors and Chrysler), produced the bulk of cars sold. Although still renown for their gas-guzzling "muscle cars", pressure from imports and domestic demand for more compact, fuel-efficient cars, led to a general downsizing. Compact and sub-compact car sales grew, increasing markedly after the Arab embargo oil crisis of 1973.

1971 was the year American muscle cars battled to maintain relevance and dominance. These high-performance coupes with large, powerful V-8 engines and rear wheel drive had been designed to satisfy our desire for power above all else. But the introduction of the Clean Air Act of 1970 forced automakers to drastically reduce emission pollutants. Clean air equipment became the new focus, robbing engines of much of their raw power and performance.

American auto makers responded to the stricter federal requirements, and to the increased competition from imports, by creating compact, more fuel-efficient car models. However poor design, engineering and manufacturing led to a stream of disasters, damaging the customer experience.

3. Result: a better sporty small car.

**The better small car.
1971 Mercury Comet GT.**

Six car-producing countries dominated the industry in 1971: Japan, Germany, England, France and Italy, with America in the top spot. Japan's recent rise into this elite group had been particularly aggressive, and their cars stood poised to dominate the world markets.

Japanese cars were reliable, affordable, compact, efficient and popular, quickly making Toyota, Nissan, Mitsubishi, Mazda and Honda the export market leaders. Japanese cars exports increased nearly 200-fold from start to end of the 60s.

Introducing the Toyota Celica ST.
(Some economy car.)

Volkswagen's Beetle remained popular, as it had been throughout the 1960s. Buyers tended to view German and Japanese cars as more reliable, safer and more fuel-efficient.

Imports of foreign cars now made up 14.6% of American new car sales.

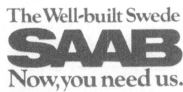

The Well-built Swede

SAAB

Now, you need us.

Today, you have good reason to see your SAAB dealer's full line of well-built Swedes.

'71 Chevelle. How do you change America's most popular mid-size car?

Very carefully. You'd be surprised at all the advice we get.

Some of it comes from our engineers, our stylists, our safety experts, our dealers, our stockholders.

Even some from people we pay solely for advice: researchers.

But a lot of it comes from you.

There's a lot you've always liked about Chevelle.

However one of the things you wanted for '71 was some new colors. We offer you 13 of them, all brand-new shades.

We contoured a new grille, and front and rear bumpers.

Again, carefully. Very carefully.

Put in new Power-Beam headlights. Single uncluttered units. Simple but effective.

Effective, too, in our drive for clean air is our new Evaporation Control System. It uses absorbent charcoal to help keep carburetor and gas-tank evaporation out of the atmosphere.

While inside we provide you a new steering wheel with a cushioned center, and new control knobs wrapped in soft vinyl.

The whole idea is to keep Chevelle as popular with you as its price is.

1971. You've changed. We've changed. Chevelle

Very carefully. You'd be surprised at all the advice we get. Some of it comes from our engineers, our stylists, our safety experts, our dealers, our stockholders. Even some from people we pay solely for advice: researchers.

But a lot of it comes from you. There's a lot you've always liked about Cheville. However one of the things you wanted for '71 was some new colors. We offer you 13 of them, all brand-new shades.

We contoured a new grille, and front and rear bumpers. Again, carefully. Very carefully. Put in new Power-Beam headlights. Single uncluttered units. Simple but effective. Effective, too, in our drive for clean air is our new Evaporation Control System. It uses absorbent charcoal to help keep carburetor and gas-tank evaporation out of the atmosphere.

While inside we provide you a new steering wheel with a cushioned center, and new control knobs wrapped in soft vinyl.

The whole idea is to keep Chevelle as popular with you as its price is.

Clean Air for All

Driver wearing a smog mask in 1970 Los Angeles, USA.

Our love affair with gas-guzzling, pollutant-emitting cars caused our air quality to deteriorate to severely unhealthy levels throughout the 50s and 60s. By the early 70s, pollutants from exhaust and industries left major cities regularly blanketed in a hazardous thick brown haze.

1971 saw the newly created US Environmental Protection Agency hand the states a short five years to clean up their air quality. The Clean Air Act (passed 31st December 1970) required a 90% reduction of emissions from new automobiles within five years, targeting six major public health pollutants, including lead and carbon monoxide.

Clean Air Act impacts

Comparison of 1970 and 2008 Emissions

CO (−59%) NOₓ (−40%) VOC (−49%) SO₂ (−62%) PM₂.₅ (−27%) Pb (−99%)

Lead Content in Gasoline and Ave Blood Lead Levels.

Key
Average Blood Lead Levels
Lead Used in Gasoline

1976 1977 1978 1979 1980

Failure to adhere to the restrictions resulted in fines and penalties to the states or cities. They, in turn, put pressure on car manufacturers to phase out leaded petrol engines and engineer cleaner, more efficient vehicles.

The UK implemented their first Clean Air Act in 1956. Their revised Act of 1970 specifically targeted carbon monoxide and hydrocarbons from automobile engines.

In Canada, Australia, and across Europe, similar legislations were developed throughout the 70s to tackle the undeniable problem of automobile-created photochemical smog which affected all major cities.

Every country set their own standards, some more stringent than others. They also created their own methods for emissions testing of vehicles prior to sale, and of air quality testing for cities.

New York aerial view in 1973 and now.

L.A. Grand Avenue in 1967 and now.

London's Great Fog of 1952 resulted in the deaths of 12,000 Londoners.

The crew of the Phyllis Cormack (also called "Greenpeace") on-board the ship. Clockwise from top left: Hunter, Moore, Cummings, Metcalfe, Birmingham, Cormack, Darnell, Simmons, Bohlen, Thurston, and Fineberg. September 1971.

On 15th September 1971, a small group of concerned activists set sail from Vancouver to the Alaskan island of Amchitka to protest US nuclear testing taking place there. While waiting near the testing site, they stumbled upon a disused fishing village and whaling station. The discarded whale bones gave them the idea for their next campaign.

The organization Greenpeace was soon formed, with the aim of merging the anti-war movement with the environmental movement. By targeting human or political actions that harm the environment, Greenpeace activists were prepared to put themselves in harms way, protesting through peaceful resistance or direct confrontation.

Greenpeace's early anti-whaling campaigns received extensive TV coverage. Activists were shown sandwiched between giant whaling trawlers and bloody harpooned whales. Membership skyrocketed.

Today Greenpeace has offices in over 40 countries, tackling diverse issues from protecting the oceans, forests and endangered animals, to fighting climate change and toxic waste dumping.

Nuclear Bomb Testing

Remember when dropping nuclear bombs was commonplace? For more than 40 years, the Nuclear Arms Race gave the USA and USSR the pretext needed to test nuclear bombs on a massive scale. Nearly 1,700 bombs were dropped by the Superpowers, most of them during the decades of the 60s and 70s. A further 300 were tested by China, France, and the UK.

On 6th Nov 1971, the US conducted its most powerful underground Nuclear explosion to date. The 5-megaton bomb was placed more than one mile below Amchitka Island in Alaska.

A partial Nuclear Test Ban Treaty in 1963 limited bomb testing in the atmosphere, in space, and under the ocean, making underground testing the standard for the next 3 decades.

These tests served to understand the effectiveness and capacity of each bomb type. They also acted as a deterrent to enemy nations.

In 1971 the US carried out 24 nuclear tests, mostly at the Nevada Proving Grounds, while USSR tested 23 nuclear bombs.

A French atmospheric nuclear test at Mururoa atoll in 1971.

Although most of the test sites were largely uninhabited by humans, some of them were densely populated. The effects of radioactive fallout plagued local populations for years afterwards.

"If I join the Women's Army Corps they'll cut off my hair."

Some girls believe the myth that the Women's Army Corps will try to make foot soldiers out of them. Cut their hair. And give them a baggy uniform.

Well, that's just plain nonsense.

Off duty or on, a girl can tint, tease, frost, iron her hair, or top it off with a new wig.

So there's never a hang-up with hair. There's even a place for your wig stand.

We know how special a girl's hair is to her total look. After all, we're girls, too. And we wouldn't dream of telling her how to wear it.

We do have one very practical rule that says hair should be kept above the collar while on duty. Just like any professional girl in uniform.

And there's one big regulation about the uniforms—that they make a girl look like one! It's her patriotic duty to stay looking trim and attractive.

A girl in the Women's Army Corps looks great because she feels great. About the world of travel, new friends, and job opportunities she's discovered.

Send the coupon, and we'll share it with you.

Or write: Army Opportunities, Department 400/450A, Hampton, Virginia 23369.

Please indicate education in your letter or coupon.

Your world is bigger in the Women's Army Corps.

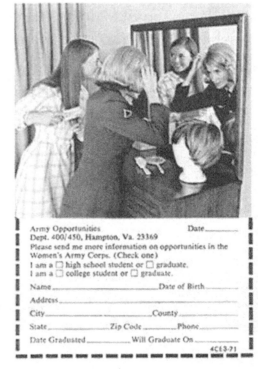

We had long ago grown tired and fed-up with the ongoing Vietnam War (known in Vietnam as the American War). By 1971, 156,800 US troops remained in Vietnam, with an additional 53,850 allied troops from South Korea, Thailand, Australia and New Zealand.[1]

Anti-war sentiment had been escalating during the previous few years, as more and more protestors took to the streets against what they believed to be an immoral war.

Numerous anti-war marches and civil disobedience campaigns were waged throughout the months of March and April, culminating with a 500,000 strong march on 24th April 1971 in Washington D.C. At the same time 150,000 marched in San Francisco.

Within weeks, the May Day protests began with the militant aim of bringing D.C. to a standstill. Protestors blocked roads, bridges and buildings. Police charged and fired tear gas, arresting 12,000 protesters over 3 days. It was the largest mass arrest in American history.

Actress Jane Fonda, the war's most high-profile critic, earned the nickname "Hanoi Jane" for her outspoken activism.

Forced to fight a war they didn't believe in, morale among the draftees was low. Drug usage became rampant. It is estimated up to 50% of US soldiers experimented with marijuana, opium and heroin, cheaply available on the streets of Saigon. US military hospitals would later report drug abuse victims far outnumbered actual war casualties.

[1] americanwarlibrary.com/vietnam/vwatl.htm.

Pentagon Papers White House Scandal June 1971

On 13th June 1971, the New York Times ran a series of leaked articles exposing the truth about US political and military involvement in Vietnam, Cambodia and Laos from 1945 to 1967. The articles were excerpts from a 3,000-page secret Department of Defense report known as the Pentagon Papers.

Among other things, the report highlighted the extent to which successive governments had systematically lied to the American people and to Congress. It traced the covert actions of the military and the CIA in Indochina under Presidents Truman, Eisenhower, Kennedy, and Johnson. It exposed the misinformation spread to the American public to keep them engaged in a war they did not wholly believe in.

Newspaper headlines from June 1971.

The New York Times printed just three articles before the Nixon administration forced the paper to cease printing. The Washington Post began publishing articles on 18th June. They were met with a similar injunction to cease printing. Meanwhile several other papers received similar leaked articles and confirmed their intent to print.

On 30th June, the Supreme Court ruled that the media could print any articles they deemed newsworthy. Charges against Daniel Ellsberg, the researcher who had leaked the report, were eventually dropped.

Space Missions of 1971

Space missions did not stall after NASA's Apollo 11 historic man-on-the-moon mission. America's claim to have won the Space Race did not stop them, or the Soviets, from ongoing space exploration. In fact, the goals simply shifted. Having conquered the moon, what was next?

NASA continued taking astronauts to the moon, successfully landing two more spacecraft during 1971.

Apollo 14 launched 9th February, becoming the third successful NASA moon mission. Astronauts Alan Shepard and Edgar Mitchell performed 9 hours of moon walks, bringing home 98 pounds of lunar material.

Crew of the Apollo 14: Stuart A. Roosa, Alan B. Shepard Jr. and Edgar D. Mitchell.

Apollo 15 launched 26th July. Astronauts Jim Iwrin and David Scott spent 67 hours on the moon's surface. A Lunar Roving Vehicle, the first of its kind, was used to collect 173 pounds of moon rock.

James Irwin salutes the American flag in front of the landing module and rover, 2nd August 1971.

Launch of Atlas-Centaur carrying Mariner 9.

NASA had also been developing robotic probes since 1963. The Mariner program had its focus on exploring Mars, Venus and Mercury.

Eight Mariner missions were carried out during the 60s to various degrees of success. Mariner 9, launched 30th May 1971, reached Mars after 6 months of traveling, becoming the first spacecraft to orbit another planet.

During its 349 days in orbit, Mariner 9 sent back over 7,000 images, mapping 85% of the surface of Mars.

The USSR abandoned plans to land on the moon after America's success in 1969. Their focus immediately shifted to developing a space station capable of supporting humans for extended periods in space. And to destinations further afield.

Diagram showing a Soyuz craft (rear) docking with the Salyut 1 (front).

The Soviet's Salyut 1 launched into low earth orbit on 19th April 1971, becoming the world's first space station. It received the 3-man crew of Soyuz 11 on 7th June. The cosmonauts remained on board for 22 days, orbiting the earth 362 times.

Within seconds of their return craft entering the Earth's atmosphere, the air-tight hatch seals failed, killing all 3 cosmonauts within.

The Salyut 1 was intentionally destroyed after 6 months in orbit, to be replaced by seven more space stations during the 15-year Salyut program. The program was vital for developing space station technology.

Soyez 11 Cosmonauts Georgy Dobrovolsky, Vladislav Volkov and Viktor Patsayev commemorated on a 1971 Soviet post stamp.

The Soviets set their goals even further when they launched two identical probes headed for Mars in March 1971. The Mars 2 and Mars 3 probes were orbiters with attached landers.

The Mars 2 lander crash-landed on Mars, loosing contact with Earth. The Mars 3 lander successfully soft-landed on 2nd Dec 1971. It transmitted for just 20 secs. It is not sure if its rover was deployed.

Diagram of Mars 2 (and identical Mars 3) orbiter with its lander on top.

Both orbiters successfully sent data and photos back to Earth from December 1971 until March 1972.

A Kindness Instant Hairsetter styles it high, wide and easy to comb, in just 15 minutes. Without hot combs or harsh chemicals.

This side was shaped with a comb.

This side was set with the Kindness Spray-and-Roll System.

"The Troubles" was a 30-year long nationalist campaign, or low-level war, waged by Northern Irish Roman Catholic Republicans against the British (Protestant) Ulster Unionists. Although often mistaken for a war of religion, it was in fact a political war. The Republicans were fighting for the reunification of Northern Ireland with the Republic of Ireland. The Unionists were determined to keep Northern Ireland as part of the United Kingdom.

The Troubles flared up in the late 60s with local violence between the two factions. British Troops arrived to quell the situation, remaining for 37 years. Although their role was to be neutral peace-keepers, they were soon condemned for covertly supporting the Unionists.

British Troops arrest a suspected Republican, 6th Aug 1971.

A section of Peace Wall.

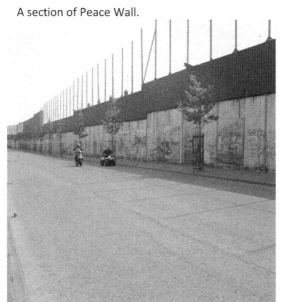

Peace Walls were hastily erected throughout the cities and suburbs of Northern Ireland, physically separating Republicans from Unionist neighborhoods.

A total of 21 miles (34 km) of Peace Walls were built by the British Government, which in recent years have become something of a tourist attraction.

A Northern Ireland commitment has been made to remove all the Peace Walls.

From 1971 to 1973 the political violence escalated. Republican paramilitaries commonly used guerilla tactics and bombing campaigns against British infrastructure, commercial and political targets, while Unionists attacked the wider Catholic community in "retaliation". A secret British Army unit, the Military Reaction Force, carried out undercover drive-by shootings against unarmed Catholic civilians.

9th August 1971– The British Government legalized internment (imprisonment without trial). Four days of violence followed resulting in the deaths of 20 civilians–all of them Catholic. Many reported physical and verbal abuse at the hands of the British troops. Many became radicalized as a result. British troops imprisoned nearly 350 people suspected of Republican paramilitary involvement under the internment laws.

Suspected Republicans rounded up for internment.

British troops during Bloody Sunday riots.

4th December 1971– Unionist paramilitaries bombed McGurk's Bar in Belfast, Northern Ireland. 15 Catholic civilians died when the building collapsed.

The bomb sparked a series of retaliatory attacks from both sides, culminating in the Bloody Sunday massacre of January 1972, when British Troops shot 26 civilians, killing 14, in full view of the public and press.

Throughout 1972, the worst year of the Troubles, nearly 500 people would lose their lives.

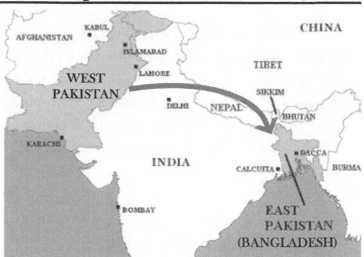

Bangladesh (formerly East Pakistan) is unique in the world, having been given a seat in the UN after unilaterally declaring independence from (West) Pakistan.

In March 1971, after 24 turbulent years in a forced union with West Pakistan, Bangladesh declared independence. Although separated by geography, politics, language and culture, the larger and more powerful western region was not prepared to release its renegade eastern state. Government forces were sent to enforce the union. Reports of mass atrocities, including genocide, changed international opinion in favor of the Bengali cause.

Pakistan Generals sign the Instrument of Surrender, 16th Dec 1971.

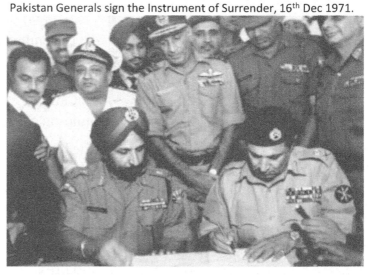

On 3rd December 1971, India entered the conflict, sending troops to assist the Bengalis. Within two weeks they had forced West Pakistan to accept defeat.

India formally recognized Bangladesh as a separate nation, leading other countries to do the same. In 1974 Bangladesh joined the UN, cementing its status as an independent country.

SPECIAL OFFER FROM KODAK.
SMILE SAVER KIT.

SPECIAL: You get a handsome, convenient travel case for your X-15.

SPECIAL: You get three self-powered Sylvania Blue Dot magicubes for twelve flash pictures.

SPECIAL: You get a Smile Saver pocket picture album.

Snap and save, now. Kodak makes this extra-special offer—for a limited time only—to introduce the camera that takes flash pictures without flash batteries. You get everything you need including Kodacolor-X film and the new Kodak Instamatic* X-15 camera. Just drop in the film. Pop on a magicube. And snap and save. A great gift idea, too.

COMPLETE GIFT OUTFIT. LESS THAN $25.

Kodak makes your pictures count.

Snap and save, now. Kodak makes this extra-special offer—for a limited time only—to introduce the camera that takes flash picture without flash batteries. You get everything you need including Kodacolor-X film and the new Kodak Instamatic X-15 camera. Just drop in the film. Pop on a magicube. And snap and save. A great gift idea, too.

Special: You get a handsome, convenient travel case for your X-15
Special: You get three self-powered Sylvania Blue Dot magicubes for twelve flash pictures.
Special: You get a Smile Saver pocket picture album.

Kodak makes your pictures count.

Death Sentence for Charles Manson

Charles Manson in custody.

On 25th January, Charles Manson and three female members of his cult "family" were found guilty of first-degree murder. They would be sentenced to death by gas chamber on 19th April.

Charles Manson was the leader of "the family", a San Francisco based hippie cult of mostly female followers. He preached an apocalyptic war he called "Helter Skelter" would soon occur, where blacks would kill all the whites leaving only his family as the rulers of the earth.

In 1969 Manson ordered his followers to start Helter Skelter. Susan Atkins, Patricia Krenwinkel, and Charles "Tex" Watson, with Linda Kasabian as their driver, were sent to the home of Hollywood actress Sharon Tate, wife of director Roman Polanski. Tate, heavily pregnant at the time, and four of her guests were brutally murdered.

Sharon Tate in 1969.

Susan Atkins, Patricia Krenwinkel, Leslie Van Houten, and Tex Watson mug shots, 1971.

The following night Manson led the same four, plus Leslie Van Houten, to another home where they murdered Leno and Rosemary LaBianca. Two days later Kasabian fled the family. She would later testify as chief witness in their murder trials.

The Tate LaBianca murderers would eventually be caught and tried. Manson carved a swastika on his forehead, while Atkins, Krenwinkel, and Van Houten laughed throughout their trial. Watson was tried separately and given a death sentence on 21st October. In 1972, all death sentences were changed to life in prison.

Tuning in to Television

The television was our must-have appliance of the mid 20th century, taking pride of place in our family or living rooms. By 1971, 95.5% of US households owned a television.[1]

Color TVs had been around since the early 50s, however very few people purchased them. Broadcasting in color did not take off until 1965. Within two years, all the networks broadcast in color. By 1971, an estimated 48% of American households owned a color TV.[2]

Although some countries, like Canada and the UK, were catching up to the US with color TV broadcasting and ownership, Australia would wait till 1975 for their first color television broadcasts.

Elsewhere in the world, rates of television ownership lagged behind the USA.

In many countries, television networks were government owned or subsidized, allowing for more focus on serious documentaries and news, without the constant concern of generating advertising revenue.

Carroll O'Connor and Mike Evans in *All in the Family* (CBS. 1971-1979).

Most Popular TV Shows of 1971 [3]

1	All in the Family	=	Here's Lucy
2	The Flip Wilson Show	12	Hawaii Five-O
3	Marcus Welby, M.D.	13	Medical Center
4	Gunsmoke	14	The NBC Mystery Movie
5	ABC Movie of the Week	15	Ironside
6	Sanford and Son	16	The Partridge Family
7	Mannix	17	The F.B.I.
8	Funny Face	18	The New Dick Van Dyke Show
=	Adam-12	19	The Wonderful World of Disney
10	The Mary Tyler Moore Show	20	Bonanza

[1] americancentury.omeka.wlu.edu/items/show/136.
[2] tvobscurities.com/articles/color60s/.
[3] Nielsen Media Research 1971-72 season of top-rated primetime television series.

Although sitcoms and variety programs remained popular in 1971, a new wave of intense TV dramas was keeping us glued to our television sets. A slew of police, detective, or medical themed primetime TV programs hit our screens in the late 60s, and we were hooked.

Eight of the twenty top-ranking TV series for 1971 were medical or crime themed programs, most lasting well into the decade.

Airing for an impressive 12 seasons, *Hawaii Five-0* was largely shot on location in Honolulu, Hawaii. It followed a special police task force fighting organized crime across the Hawaiian Islands.

Jack Lord, Al Harrington, Kam Fong and James MacArthur in *Hawaii Five-0* (CBS. 1968-1980).

The original series ended in 1980. A 2010 remake, based on the original series, is now in its 10th season.

Robert Young as Marcus Welby, with James Brolin as his head-strong young assistant and Elena Verdugo as their nurse, in *Marcus Welby, M.D.* (ABC. 1969-1976).

The Sonny & Cher Comedy Hour
(CBS. 1971-1974).

Dick Van Dyke, Hope Lange, Angela Powell &
Michael Shea in *The New Dick Van Dyke Show*
(CBS. 1971-1974).

The television networks were quick to turn out new programs to keep us tuning in. Here are a few of the new programs that aired for the first time in 1971: *All in the Family, The Sonny & Cher Comedy Hour, The New Dick Van Dyke Show, Columbo,* and *The Jackson 5ive.* Other notables include *The Two Ronnies,* and *Parkinson* (both BBC1, UK).

Peter Falk in *Columbo* (NBC. 1971-1978).

Ronnie Barker and Ronnie Corbett in
The Two Ronnies (BBC1. 1971-1987).

This year's sale is something very special.

But then this year's sets are something very special.

This year's sale is special because it includes over 75 of the best 1971 color TV and stereo sets we make.

Not just a few leftover models.

This year's color TVs are special because they have the sharpest big screen picture tube ever made. Some even have our new instant pushbutton tuner, and 100% solid-state Gibraltar chassis.

This year's console stereos are special because they all have air suspension speakers. Precision turntables. Powerful amplifiers. And sensitive AM/FM tuners.

The portable stereos are special because they're inexpensive to begin with.

So if you want something very special—and you want to save a lot of money—drop in to your nearest Sylvania dealer.

But do it now. Remember, some sales really do end.

SYLVANIA
GENERAL TELEPHONE & ELECTRONICS

Walt Disney World Opens 1

With the highly successful Disneyland theme park in California now 16 years old, Walt Disney Company's second theme park opened on 1st October 1971 in Orlando, Florida.

Thousands of balloons released to celebrate Walt Disney World's grand opening.

The Magic Kingdom with performers.

The original 1971 Magic Kingdom park with two hotels has now grown into a cluster of 4 themed parks plus 2 water parks, and over 25 resort hotels. The expansions continue to bring in new attractions while constantly upgrading existing favorites.

Although Walt Disney died in 1966 during the initial stages of planning, his brother and business partner, Roy O. Disney, worked tirelessly to ensure Walt's dream would come to fruition. Roy died just three months after the park's opening at 78 years old.

Jesus Christ Superstar on Broadway 12ᵗʰ October 1971

Composed by a very young Andrew Lloyd Webber, with lyrics by Tim Rice, the rock-opera theatrical sensation *Jesus Christ Superstar* was first released as a concept album a year before its stage debut on Broadway in October 1971. It won Webber a Drama Desk Award for the *Most Promising Composer*, which was to prove well earned. He would become one of musical theatre's most celebrated composers, with mega-hits such as *Phantom of the Opera, Cats, Evita*, and *School of Rock*.

Andrew Lloyd Webber receives Kennedy Center Honors in 2006.

Told through the eyes of Judas Iscariot, the musical's controversial interpretation of Jesus' last few days on earth, the compassion given to Judas, and the portrayal of the Jews as the villains, caused the musical to be condemned by many religious groups and banned in some countries.

Photos from the original Broadway cast of 1971.
Left: Roman soldiers carrying Jesus.
Right: Judas with Pharisees.

Scene from the last supper.

The production would open in London the following year with sell-out shows, becoming the longest running musical on the West End at that time.

Since then, the *Jesus Christ Superstar* has been translated and performed on stage and in arenas around the world. It has also been showcased several times on TV and on film.

1971 in Cinema and Film

As cinema-going viewers, our interests and focus had turned away from traditional classic Hollywood mainstays, bounding with optimism and happy endings. We yearned for more reality, more depth.

By 1971, a new breed of directors like Francis Ford Coppola and Martin Scorsese demanded more artistic control. They bravely tackled darker, more gritty and more pessimistic themes of war, crime and depression. The era of big cinema houses owning their actors and controlling their directors had ended.

A new generation of brooding method-style actors rose to replace the retiring golden-era stars. Dustin Hoffman, Robert De Niro, Meryl Streep, Al Pacino, Jack Nicholson and Harvey Keitel are some of our enduring favorites.

Al Pacino in *Panic in Needle Park* (20th Century Fox, 1971).

Jack Nicholson and Candice Bergen in *Carnal Knowledge* (Embassy Pictures, 1971).

1971 film debuts

Kathy Bates	Taking Off
Stockard Channing	The Hospital
Daniel Day-Lewis	Sunday Bloody Sunday
Gérard Depardieu	Cry of the Cormoran
Cybill Shepherd	The Last Picture Show
Jacki Weaver	Stork

* From en.wikipedia.org/wiki/1971_in_film.

Top Grossing Films of the Year

1	Fiddler on the Roof	United Artists	$40,500,000
2	Billy Jack	Warner Bros.	$32,500,000
3	The French Connection	20th Century Fox	$26,300,000
4	Summer of '42	Warner Bros.	$20,500,000
5	Diamonds Are Forever	United Artists	$19,727,000
6	Dirty Harry	Warner Bros.	$18,000,000
7	A Clockwork Orange	Warner Bros.	$17,000,000
8	Carnal Knowledge	Embassy Pictures	$14,075,000
9	The Last Picture Show	Columbia Pictures	$13,110,000
10	Willard	Cinerama Releasing Corp.	$9,300,000

* From en.wikipedia.org/wiki/1971_in_film by box office gross in the USA.

Stanley Kubrick's disturbing dystopian crime film *A Clockwork Orange* won the New York Film Critics Award, despite sexually explicit scenes causing it to be banned in numerous countries.

The French Connection won five out of eight Oscar nominations, including Best Picture, Best Director (for William Friedkin), and Best Actor (for Gene Hackman).

A Decade of Disasters

The Poseidon Adventure
(20th Century Fox, 1972).

The Towering Inferno
(20th Century Fox, 1974).

The decade of the 70s saw the disaster movie genre reign supreme at the box office. Large casts, multiple plot lines, life or death calamities and tales of survival kept us on the edge of our seats.

Earthquake (Universal, 1974).

Tidalwave (Toho, 1973).

Musical Memories

1971 was a golden year for rock. The Beatles had just split up, we had turned our backs on 60s psychedelic rock and silly love songs, and some of the most influential music and albums of our lifetime were recorded. Musicians were writing, recording, and performing at a blistering pace.

A new generation of singer-songwriters were penning lyrics about serious social and personal issues. Carole King's *Tapestry* stayed at #1 on Billboard for 15 weeks. Joni Mitchell's *Blue* was listed #3 on *Rolling Stone* magazine's *500 Greatest Albums of All Time* (2020). Led Zeppelin's *IV,* featuring their signature song *Stairway to Heaven*, defined the mood and style of 70's Hard Rock.

Other influential records included *Who's Next* by The Who, *Master of Reality* by Black Sabbath, *L.A. Women* by The Doors, *Sticky Fingers* by The Rollings Stones, *Every Picture Tells A Story* by Rod Stewart, *Carly Simon* by Carly Simon, and *American Pie* by Don McLean.

Marvin Gaye's groundbreaking album *What's Going On* explored hatred, suffering, injustice, poverty and drug abuse from the viewpoint of a returning Vietnam Vet. It was a marked departure from the usual Motown sound.

John Lennon's single *Imagine* was released on 8th October, from the album of the same name. It would become the biggest selling single of his solo career and an enduring anthem of peace, love and social change.

The first Glastonbury Festival (Somerset, UK) was held from 20th-24th June to coincide with the summer solstice. Money was put up and the land provided to ensure the event remained free to festival goers.

The temperamental British weather remained largely fine as a crowd of 7,000 gathered. Although not considered huge, the festival was a success, with David Bowie headlining the twenty-act line-up.

As the festival was not a money-making affair, it would not become a yearly event until the 1980s.

The signature steel-structure pyramid stage, first erected in 1971, continues to appear today in modified and updated forms.

At the same time, the Celebration of Life festival in McCrae (Louisiana, USA) suffered untold disasters. Poor organization left the site unsecured till 4 days before the event. None of the promised big-name acts showed up, reducing the eight-day festival to just four days.

An abundance of drugs and mosquitoes, and lack of toilets, food and water, made conditions unbearable. The extreme heat forced bands to perform only at night. Gale force winds blew down part of the stage. And at day's end, three were dead from drugs and drowning.

In other news:

12th May– Mick Jagger married Bianca Pérez-Mora Macías in Paris.

3rd Jul– Jim Morrison, aged 27, was found dead in his bathtub in Paris. The official cause of death was heart failure, although numerous eyewitnesses believe an accidental heroin overdose was to blame.

1971 Billboard Top 30 Songs

	Artist	Song Title
1	Three Dog Night	Joy to the World
2	Rod Stewart	Maggie May / Reason to Believe
3	Carole King	It's Too Late / I Feel the Earth Move
4	The Osmonds	One Bad Apple
5	Bee Gees	How Can You Mend a Broken Heart
6	Paul Revere & the Raiders	Indian Reservation
7	Donny Osmond	Go Away Little Girl
8	John Denver	Take Me Home, Country Roads
9	The Temptations	Just My Imagination (Running Away with Me)
10	Tony Orlando and Dawn	Knock Three Times

Rod Stuart, 1971.

The Osmonds, 1971.

John Denver, 1973.

The Bee Gees, 1973.

	Artist	Song Title
11	Janis Joplin	Me and Bobby McGee
12	Al Green	Tired of Being Alone
13	Honey Cone	Want Ads
14	The Undisputed Truth	Smiling Faces Sometimes
15	Cornelius Brothers & Sister Rose	Treat Her Like a Lady
16	James Taylor	You've Got a Friend
17	Jean Knight	Mr. Big Stuff
18	The Rolling Stones	Brown Sugar
19	Lee Michaels	Do You Know What I Mean
20	Joan Baez	The Night They Drove Old Dixie Down

Tom Jones, 1969.

The Carpenters, 1972.

21	Marvin Gaye	What's Going On
22	Paul & Linda McCartney	Uncle Albert/Admiral Halsey
23	Bill Withers	Ain't No Sunshine
24	Five Man Electrical Band	Signs
25	Tom Jones	She's a Lady
26	Murray Head & The Trinidad Singers	Superstar
27	The Free Movement	I've Found Someone of My Own
28	Jerry Reed	Amos Moses
29	The Grass Roots	Temptation Eyes
30	The Carpenters	Superstar

* From the *Billboard* top 30 singles of 1971.

The either-or stereo from JVC

Model 4344 is the latest pacesetter from JVC. With more features, more versatility than any other compact in its field. You can enjoy either its superb FM stereo/AM receiver. Or your favorite albums on its 4-speed changer. Or 4-track cassettes on its built-in player. Or you can record your own stereo cassettes direct from the radio, or use its microphones (included) to record from any outside source. And you get all these great components in a beautiful wooden cabinet that can sit on a book-shelf.

But don't let its size fool you — JVC's 4344 is a real heavyweight. With 45 watts music power, 2-way speaker switching and matching air suspension speakers, illuminated function indicators, handsome blackout dial, separate bass and treble controls, FM-AFC switch. Even two VU meters to simplify recording, and more.

See the Model 4344 at your nearest JVC dealer today. Or write us direct for his address and color brochure.

JVC Catching On Fast

JVC America, Inc., 50-35, 56th Road, Maspeth, New York, N.Y. 11378

Model 4344 is the latest pacesetter from JVC. With more features, more versatility than any other compact in its field. You can enjoy either its superb FM stereo/AM receiver. Or your favorite albums on its 4-speed changer. Or 4-track cassettes on its built-in player. Or you can record your own stereo cassettes direct from the radio, or use its microphones (included) to record from any outside source. And you get all these great components in a beautiful wooden cabinet that can sit on a book-shelf.

But don't let its size fool you—JVC's 4344 is a real heavyweight. With 45 watts music power, 2-way speaker switching and matching air suspension speakers, illuminated function indicators, handsome blackout dial, separate bass and treble controls, FM-AFC switch. Even two VU meters to simplify recording, and more.

See the Model 4344 at your nearest JVC dealer today. Or write us direct for his address and color brochure.

How to kill yourself.

Eat! Drink! And Be Merry?

And whatever you do, by all means, overdo it.

Eat! It gives you something to do when you're bored or tense. (Sure, your doctor told you how many calories you should take in in a day. But it's been a long day.)

Drink! You don't really need it to unwind. It's just to be sociable.

A second helping of dessert? Lemon meringue pie is mostly egg white. And how about a pizza while you are watching TV after dinner? Of course, it always tastes better with beer.

What was it your doctor said? "People are the only animals who eat themselves to death." But you know it's your glands, not your appetite, that makes *you* plump.

Why Are America's Doctors Telling You This?

Well, for a long time we've been telling you how to stay alive and healthy. (Last year, 70% of the annual budget of the American Medical Association went to health and scientific education.) But many of you go do the opposite.

Now we figure we'll tell you how to kill yourselves. In the fervent hope that once again you'll do the exact opposite. If you do, there's every chance we'll be seeing less of you. Once a year for a checkup. And that's it.

Doing your bit to take care of yourself simply means your doctor can give everyone the best care possible. When *only* his care will do.

For a free booklet on eating and good health, write: American Medical Association, Box H, 535 North Dearborn Street, Chicago, Illinois 60610.

America's Doctors of Medicine
(Our Best Patients Take Care of Themselves)

Eat! Drink! And Be Merry? And whatever you do, by all means, overdo it.

Eat! It gives you something to do when you're bored or tense. (Sure, your doctor told you how many calories you should take in in a day. But it's been a long day.)

Drink! You don't really need it to unwind. It's just to be sociable.

A second helping of dessert? Lemon meringue pie is mostly egg white. And how about a pizza while you are watching TV after dinner? Of course, it always tastes better with beer. What was it your doctor said? "People are the only animals who eat themselves to death." But you know it's your glands, not your appetite, that makes *you* plump.

Why Are America's Doctors Telling You This?

Well, for a long time we've been telling you how to stay alive and healthy. (Last year, 70% of the annual budget of the American medical Association went to health and scientific education.) But many of you go do the opposite. Now we figure we'll tell you how to kill yourselves. In the fervent hope that once again you'll do the exact opposite. If you do, there's every chance we'll be seeing less of you. Once a year for a checkup. And that's it. Doing your bit to take care of yourself simply means your doctor can give everyone the best care possible. When *only* his care will do.

Fashion Trends of the 1970s

By the early 70s in the world of fashion, we had clearly lost our way and were looking for answers. This was a decade without guidance and without rules. Trends caught on and shifted quickly. Fashions were varied and experimental. Pants got wider, skirts got shorter, boots got taller. And within a season the trends reversed. Anything was possible, everything was acceptable.

Walking down any street you would have found skirts worn mini, midi, or full length. Pants could be slim-fit, wide, or bell bottomed, hip-hugging or waist-clinching. Tops might be tie-dye swirl-patterned or bold solids. Shirts came long and loose, or tight and tailored.

Daywear pants-suit and skirt-suit.

Dresses came in all shapes and lengths too. They could be short Mod shifts, or calico lace prairie-style. They could be tailored with shirt-style collars and buttoned-down fronts. They could be long and loose caftans, flowing maxi-dresses, or waisted tailored-cut with belts and A-line skirts taken straight from the 50s.

Patchwork maxi-dresses
by Yves Saint Laurent.

The hippie and psychedelic fashions of the late 60s were adopted and modified by mainstream non-hippies into more elegant structured forms. Caftans, prairie dresses, patchwork fabrics, shawls, tassels and beads hit the runways, and the streets, in the early 70s.

Elizabeth Taylor during her bohemian period, 1969.

Multicolor caftan dress.

Balestra dress, Vogue Italia, February 1970.

In contrast to the hippie trends, Mod dresses of the early 60s made a comeback. Space-age synthetics and plastics, widely used in the 60s, were replaced with comfortable cottons and stretch knits. In winter, tunic dresses could be worn over turtlenecks, with woolen stockings or thigh-high boots.

Mod mini dresses worn with white boots or shoes, early 1970s.

The 70s were the first full decade where pants for women gained mainstream acceptance, and we couldn't get enough of them. Pants could be worn for any occasion–pants-suits for the office, silky patterns for evenings, or blocks and geometrics dressed down for daywear. And let's not forget blue jeans, the staple of casualwear for both men and women.

Day wear pants from the Sears Spring/ Summer catalog, 1970.

In the early 70s men and women wore their pants gently flared at the base. As the decade wore on, the flares got wider and wider, exploding into bell-bottoms by the mid-70s.

Embroidered denim.

Flared Dacron polyester pants.

Flared silky jumpsuits.

"There's a new man in my life."

People think a bachelor girl like me has lots of men in her life. And I do. There's the milkman. The mailman. The laundry man. And now, there's a new man in my life... the Car Man at CITGO.

The Car man does more than just fill the tank with gasoline. He explains things to me. He told me that you rotate the tires for the same reason you flip a mattress. So they don't wear out in one place. The Car Man looks for trouble, too. The kind of trouble a woman doesn't even know can happen. Like when you don't change the oil.

The Car Man takes care of my whole car. And that makes me feel a lot better about driving. I just don't know what a girl like me would do without him. I think the Car Man makes CITGO an even nicer place to visit.

There's a Car Man for every woman at CITGO.

Shiny polyester Nik Nik shirts.   Stretch polyester tops and pants.   Terry toweling jumpsuits.

Caught between the hippie and mod extremes of early 70s fashion, the rest of us settled for easy-care. Whether casual, formal or business attire, being easy to wash and drip-dry dictated what we wore. Non-iron wool jersey knits and non-iron polyester were the material of choice for men and women throughout the 70s.

The 70s are often considered to be the decade that fashion forgot (or the decade of fashion that we would rather forget). And it's not hard to see why. Anything and everything became acceptable, no matter how outlandish or mismatched.

Here are some of our more questionable fashion decisions from the decade.

Shiny stretch
polyester jumpsuits.   Denim on denim.   Stretch knit pantsuits.   Safari suits.

John Travolta in *Saturday Night Fever*, 1977.

Dancer at Studio 54, New York.

And then there was disco.
It shone so brightly. It glittered so briefly.
And in a flash, it was gone.

Model wears sequined jumpsuit.

Dancers at Studio 54, New York.

Sporting silver lamé jumpsuits.

It takes beautiful close-up color portraits because that's all it takes.

Big faces—the kind of pictures you want most. The Polaroid Big Shot Land camera is only for close-up color portraits. That's why the camera looks so unusual—its length takes the place of expensive cameras with complicated lenses or special attachments. Pictures are almost all face, the kind you get in portrait studios.

Portraits that you can't mess up. Forget words like "focus" and "exposure." This is the simplest of all systems. You focus with your feet. Just walk toward your subject until the two faces in the window are one—and press the button.

Do not worry about lighting. It is the same, indoors and out. A flashcube behind a big diffusion panel gives you soft portrait lighting every shot. There are no settings. Not even batteries.

The timer signals when your picture is developed and ready to see—and that's it. So easy the kids can take <u>your</u> portrait.

Polaroid's $19.95*Big Shot.
If you can find one, Merry Christmas.

Big faces–the kind of pictures you want most. The Polaroid Big Shot Land camera is only for close-up color portraits. That's why the camera looks so unusual–its length takes the place of expensive cameras with complicated lenses or special attachments. Pictures are almost all face, the kind you get in portrait studios.

Portraits that you can't mess up. Forget words like "focus" and "exposure." This is the simplest of all systems. You focus with your feet. Just walk toward your subject until the two faces in the window are one–and press the button.

Do not worry about lighting. It is the same, indoors and out. A flashcube behind a big diffusion panel gives you soft portrait lighting every shot. There are no settings. Not even batteries.

The timer signals when your picture is developed and ready to see–and that's it. SO easy the kids can take <u>your</u> portrait.

Also in Sports

2nd Jan– 66 football supporters were crushed to death in a stairwell at Ibrox Stadium (Glasgow, Scotland) as they tried to leave following a Rangers v Celtic match. A further 200 were injured.

5th Jan– The first one-day cricket international was played at Melbourne's MCG. Australia beat England by five wickets. The match was invented as a one-off event, after 3 days of rain forced the cancellation of a Test match.

8th Mar– Known as the "Fight of the Century", the highly anticipated battle between the two undefeated champions, Joe Frazier and Muhammad Ali, at Madison Square Garden, NYC, saw Frazier end Ali's 31-fight winning streak, (Ali had not fought since 1966). Frazer won in 15 rounds to retain the heavyweight boxing title.

3rd Jun– Imran Khan made his test cricket debut for Pakistan against England at Edgbaston, UK. (5, 0-36, 0-19).

Evonne Goolagong in 1971.

June-July– Australia ruled the summer in tennis with all-Australian Women's finals at the French Open (Evonne Goolagong beat Helen Gourlay, Women's Singles), and at Wimbledon (Evonne Goolagong beat Margaret Court, Women's Singles). Australia also won the Wimbledon Men's Singles (John Newcombe beat American Stan Smith).

American Tennis champion Billie Jean King became the first female athlete to earn over $100,000 in prize money in a single year. Despite her large paychecks, King fought tirelessly to secure equal prize money for men and women.

You've probably been waiting to buy an electric watch for years. But the price stopped you. Now it won't. Because now you can have an Electric Timex at a beautiful price. Just $25. (And you can have just about any of the same styles with an automatic calendar for just $30.)

And you'll have all the benefits the name implies:

Electric accuracy.

The convenience of a watch that never needs winding. (A tiny replaceable energy cell powers the Electric Timex with steady electric accuracy for a whole year.)

A rugged watch that's water resistant and dust resistant.

And a choice of styles.

You've been waiting for an affordable price? Now you have it.

Invention of the Electronic Mail

Of all the possibilities that the internet offers us, email remains the most widely used and arguably the most important application available. Just about everybody has one or more email addresses, and most individuals and business rely on email to maintain normal daily function.

Long before we had personal computers on every desk, email had already been invented. In 1971, Ray Tomlinson, working for Bolt Beranek and Newman, developed a way to send messages between users of different computers through a network known as ARPANET, (the precursor to the modern internet).

The first electronic mail was sent between these two adjacent PDP-10 computers at BBN Technologies (connected only through the ARPANET).

Ray Tomlinson in 2004.

Tomlinson selected the "at" symbol to separate the user's name from the computer's name.

With the invention of the World Wide Web, email became available and affordable to all. Usage exploded as hundreds of millions discovered the simplicity and benefits of communicating electronically.

Other News from 1971

2nd Jan– Cigarette advertising was banned from TV in the USA.

8th Feb– The NASDAQ stock exchange commenced trading as the world's first fully-automated electronic stock market.

9th Feb– A 6.6 magnitude earthquake in the San Fernando Valley killed 64 people, leaving $500 million in property damage.

San Fernando highway overpass collapse, 1971.

5th Apr– Mount Etna (Sicily, Italy), Europe's largest volcano, erupted at 7.30pm. Molten lava continued to spew from numerous fissures until mid-June, flowing up to 7.5 km away.

1st Jul– Debt raised to build San Francisco's Golden Gate Bridge was finally paid off. The funds were raised through construction bonds and paid for entirely by toll charges collected on the bridge.

1st Jul– The US lowered the voting age to 18-years-old.

1st Jul– Britain and Argentina signed an accord breaking the deadlock on communications, education, and medical supplies to the Falkland Islands. The UK continued its claim of sovereignty.

8th Sep– The John F. Kennedy Center for Performing Arts opened in Washington, D.C. with a gala performance and Requiem mass in honor of the late President Kennedy.

29th Sep– A cyclone and tidal wave off the Bay of Bengal killed as many as 10,000 on the eastern coast of India. The 6-foot tidal surge reached 30 miles inland, destroying electrical and telecommunication lines, roads, crops, and tens of thousands of houses.

12th Oct– The US House of Representatives approved the Equal Rights Amendment (1971) providing legal equality for women and banning discrimination based on sex. It was passed by Senate in March 1972.

21st Oct– The Nobel prize for literature was awarded to Chilean poet Pablo Neruda, two years before his sudden death. His official cause of death was listed as heart attack however it is widely believed he was murdered by the Pinochet regime.

31st Oct– Swiss women voted for the first time after gaining suffrage in February 1971.

21st Dec– The United Arab Emirates (UAE) was formed as a union of seven small kingdoms, gaining independence from the United Kingdom after nearly 80 years of British rule. The UAE is now famed for its natural reserves of oil and gas, and extremely wealthy and modern cities.

Famous People Born in 1971

17th Jan– Kid Rock (Robert James Ritchie), American rapper, songwriter, musician & actor.

20th Jan– Gary Barlow, English singer (Take That).

22nd Feb– Lea Salonga, Filipina singer & actress.

27th Mar– Mariah Carey, American singer.

31st Mar– Ewan McGregor, Scottish actor.

12th Apr– Shannen Doherty, American actress.

14th May– Sofia Coppola, American film director.

27th May– Paul Bettany, English actor.

28th May– Marco Rubio, American politician.

30th May– Idina Menzel, American actress & singer.

5th Jun– Mark Wahlberg, actor & rapper.

22nd Jun– Kurt Warner, American Pro Football Hall of Fame quarterback.

26th Jun– Max Biaggi, Italian Grand Prix motorcycle racer.

27th Jun– Jo Frost, British TV personality (Supernanny).

28th Jun– Elon Musk, American entrepreneur & inventor.

3rd Jul– Julian Assange, Australian founder of Wikileaks.

20th Jul– Sandra Oh, Korean Canadian actress.

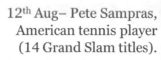

12th Aug– Pete Sampras, American tennis player (14 Grand Slam titles).

20th Aug– David Walliams, English actor, comedian & children's author.

31st Aug– Chris Tucker, American stand-up comedian & actor.

8th Sep– David Arquette, American actor, director & producer.

8th Sep– Martin Freeman, English actor.

8th Sep– Lachlan Murdoch, Australian, British, American businessman (New Corp) & son of Rupert Murdoch.

13th Sep– Goran Ivanišević, Croatian tennis player.

13th Sep– Stella Nina McCartney, English fashion designer & daughter of Paul McCartney

16th Sep– Amy Poehler, American comedian & actress.

18th Sep– Lance Armstrong, American road cyclist (7 Tour de France titles) banned for illegal drug use.

18th Sep– Jada Pinkett Smith, American actress.

13th Oct– Sacha Baron Cohen, British comedian & actor.

20th Oct– Snoop Dogg [Calvin Broadus], American rapper.

29th Oct– Winona Ryder, American actress.

21st Nov– Michael Strahan, American Pro Football Hall of Fame & TV host.

1971 in Numbers

Census Statistics [1]

- Population of the world   3.78 billion
- Population in the United States   211.38 million
- Population in the United Kingdom   55.75 million
- Population in Canada   21.72 million
- Population in Australia   13.03 million
- Average age for marriage of women   20.9 years old
- Average age for marriage of men   23.1 years old
- USA divorce rate   37%
- Average family income USA $9,030 per year
- Minimum wage USA $1.60 per hour

Costs of Goods [2]

- Average new house $25,250
- Average new car $3,500
- Chevrolet Pickup $2,229
- A gallon of gasoline $0.36
- A loaf of bread $0.25
- A gallon of milk $1.32
- Frozen french fries $0.69 per 5 pounds
- Sliced bacon $0.69 per pound
- Fresh turkey $0.69 per pound
- Potatoes $0.12 per pound
- Fresh eggs $0.53 per dozen
- Peanut butter $0.59
- A cinema ticket $1.65
- US Postage stamp $0.08

[1] Figures taken from worldometers.info/world-population, US National Center for Health Statistics, *Divorce and Divorce Rates* US (cdc.gov/nchs/data/series/sr_21/sr21_029.pdf) and United States Census Bureau, *Historical Marital Status Tables* (census.gov/data/tables/time-series/demo/families/marital.html).
[2] Figures from thepeoplehistory.com and mclib.info/reference/local-history-genealogy/historic-prices/1971-2/.

Image Attributions

Photographs and images used in this book are reproduced courtesy of the following:

Page 4 – Advertisement from *Life* Magazine 3rd Sept 1971. Source: books.google.com/books?id=SkAEAAAAMBAJ&printsec. Pre 1978, no copyright mark (Public Domain (PD*) image).
Page 6&7 – PD images from the U.S. News & World Report collection at the Library of Congress Prints and Photo division.
Page 8 – Advertisement from *Life* Magazine 3rd Sept 1971. Source: books.google.com/books?id=SkAEAAAAMBAJ&printsec. Pre 1978, no copyright mark (PD* image).
Page 9 – Photos circa 1971, creators unknown. Sources: reddit.com/r/OldSchoolCool/comments/890bq6/ and daemen.edu/about/give-daemen/founders-celebration-events/college-history-timeline. Pre 1978, no renewed copyright.
Page 10 – Photos unknown dates and creators. Sources: footage.framepool.com/shotimg/524716167. Pre 1978, no copyright mark (PD image) and jimmysirrelslovechild.co.uk/fans/stoke-1970. Pre 1978, no copyright mark (PD image).
Page 11 – Women's Liberation protest 8th Nov 1971. Source: redflagwalks.wordpress.com/category/womens-liberation/. Pre 1978 (PD image). – Boy crossing road, date and creator unknown. Pre 1978, no copyright mark (PD image).
Page 12 – Advertisement from *Life* Magazine 8th Jan 1971. Source: books.google.com/books?id=nFMEAAAAMBAJ&printsec. Pre 1978, no copyright mark (PD* image). – Decimal Day posters from Woolworths and British Rail. Sources: woolworthsmuseum.co.uk/1970s-decimalisation.html and nationalarchives.gov.uk/education/resources/significant-events/british-rail-goes-decimal-1971/. Pre 1978, no copyright mark (PD image). – Industrial Relations protest, creator unknown. Pre 1978, no copyright mark (PD image). – Engineers strike, 1973, creator unknown. Pre 1978, no copyright mark (PD image).
Page 14 – Commune members, source: allthatsinteresting.com/hippie-communes. – Tom and Pilar Law at Woodstock photo by Henry Diltz. Source: theguardian.com/music/gallery/2019/aug/15/woodstock-at-50-three-days-of-peace-pictures. Pre 1978.
Page 15 – Tending to the fields, source: burlingtonfreepress.com/story/news/local/vermont/2015/07/24/vermont-remains-hippie-epicenter/30564907/, photo by Rebecca Lepkoff of Vermont Historical Society. Pre 1978.
– Geodesic dome, source: vpr.org/post/communes-hippie-invasion-and-how-1970s-changed-state#stream/0 by Kate Daloz. Pre 1978. – Commune bus, source: allthatsinteresting.com/hippie-communes. Pre 1978. (PD image).
Page 16 – Source: flickr.com/photos/91591049@N00/25556659600/ by SenseiAlan. Attribution 4.0 Internat. (CC BY 4.0).
Page 17 – Boston Traffic in 1971, creator unknown. Source: newenglanddiary.com/home/tag/Boston+traffic. Pre 1978.
Page 18 – 1971 Dodge Demon 340 and 1971 Mercury Comet GT, source: flickr.com/photos/91591049@N00/12363684144/ and flickr.com/photos/91591049@N00/22547999418/ by SenseiAlan. Attribution 4.0 International (CC BY 4.0). – 1971 Vega by Chevrolet from *Life* 5th March 1971. Source: books.google.com/books?id=31MEAAAAMBAJ&printsec (PD* image).
Page 19 – 1971 Datsun 240-Z and 1971 Saab by SenseiAlan, source: flickr.com/photos/91591049@N00/48487590496/ and flickr.com/photos/91591049@N00/26342605796/. Attribution 4.0 International (CC BY 4.0). – 1971 Toyota from *Life* Magazine 5th Nov. Source: books.google.com/books?id=FkAEAAAAMBAJ&printsec. Pre 1978, no mark (PD* image).
Page 20 – Source: flickr.com/photos/91591049@N00/24957417155/ by SenseiAlan. Attribution 4.0 Internat. (CC BY 4.0).
Page 21 – From *Life* Magazine 1st Oct 1971. Source: books.google.com/books?id=B0AEAAAAMBAJ& printsec. (PD* image).
Page 22 – Source: latimes.com/local/california/la-me-lopez-la-better-worse-20180825-story. Pre 1978. – Chart: epa.gov/transportation-air-pollution-and-climate-change/accomplishments-and-success-air-pollution-transportation.
Page 23 – Source: insider.com/vintage-photos-los-angeles-smog-pollution-epa-2020-1. – commons.wikimedia.org/wiki/File:Two_California_Plaza_-_350_S._Grand_Avenue,_Los_Angeles. – commons.wikimedia.org/wiki/File:EAST_RIVER_AND_MANHATTAN_SKYLINE_IN_HEAVY_SMOG_-_NARA_-_548365. – quora.com/What-does-the-British-phrase-it-was-a-real-pea-souper-mean. All images pre 1978 (PD images).
Page 24 – Greenpeace founders by Robert Keziere, source: www-dev.greenpeace.org/test-uranus/about/our-history/.
Page 25 – Amchitka Island nuclear test, source: nationalinterest.org/blog/the-buzz/the-story-project-cannikin-1971-the-us-miltiary-nuked-alaska-21564. – Mururoa Atoll test, source: britannica.com/topic/Jackson-State-University (PD images).
Page 26 – Advertisement by US Women's Army Corps. Pre 1978, no copyright mark (PD) image.
Page 27 – PD images from the U.S. News & World Report collection at the Library of Congress Prints and Photo division. – Jane Fonda, press conference 18th Jan 1975. Source: commons.wikimedia. org/wiki/File:Jane_Fonda_ 1975c by Mieremet, Rob / Anefo. From the Dutch National Archives (PD image).
Page 29 – Advertisement from *Life* Magazine 7th May 1971. Source: books.google.com/books?id=LUAEAAAAMBAJ& printsec. Pre 1978, no copyright mark (PD* image).
Page 30 – Apollo 14 crew, by NASA. Source: nasa.gov/image-feature/apollo-14-crew-portrait (PD image). – Apollo 15 with Rover, by NASA. Source: nasa.gov/centers/marshall/history/this-week-in-nasa-history-apollo-15-astronauts-deploy-first-lunar-roving-vehicle-july.html (PD image). – Atlas-Centaur carrying Mariner 9 by the US Air Force. Source: en.wikipedia.org/wiki/Mariner_9#/media/File:Atlas_I-CENTAUR.jpg (PD image).
Page 31– Salyut 1 by NASA/David S. F. Portree, NASA Reference Publication 1357 (March 1995) (PD image). – Soviet stamp, 1971. Source: en.wikipedia.org/wiki/Soyuz_11 (PD image). – Mars 3 source: en.wikipedia.org/wiki/Mars_3 (PD image).
Page 32 – Salem Advertisement, source: ebay. Creator unknown. Pre 1978, no copyright mark (PD) image.
Page 33 – Source: pinterest.com.au/pin/333196072430850347/. Pre 1978, no copyright mark (PD) image.
Page 34 & 35 – Republican arrests, creators unknown. Source: anphoblacht.com/contents/26282. Pre 1978, no copyright mark (PD images). – Peace Wall by Robin Kirk, 2008. Source: flickr.com/photos/rightsatduke/4595426547/. Attribution 4.0 International (CC BY 4.0). – Bloody Sunday riots, creator unknown. Source: britainfirst.org/army_northern_ireland_veterans_stitched_up_and_sold_down_the_river. Pre 1978, no copyright mark (PD images).
Page 36 – Pakistan surrender, source: commons.wikimedia.org/wiki/Category:Bangladesh_Liberation_War (PD image).
Page 37 – Advertisement from *Life* Magazine 7th May 1971. Source: books.google.com/books?id=LUAEAAAAMBAJ& printsec. Pre 1978, no copyright mark (PD* image).
Page 38 – Manson, by Mitch Hell. Source: flickr.com/photos/64162818@N04/6301022922. Attribution-NoDerivatives 4.0 International (CC BY-ND 4.0). – Sharon Tate, source: commons.wikimedia.org/wiki/Category:Sharon_Tate (PD image).
Page 39 – Advertisement from *Life* Magazine 6th August 1971. Source: books.google.com/books?id=QUAEAAAAMBAJ& printsec. Pre 1978, no copyright mark (PD* image).
Page 40 – *All in the Family*, 4th May 1971, by CBS Television. Source: en.wikipedia.org/wiki/All_in_the_Family#/media/File:Archie_and_Lionel_All_in_the_Family_1971.JPG. Pre 1978, no copyright mark (PD image).
Page 41 – Still image and poster from the TV series *Hawaii Five-0* by CBS, 1970. These are low-resolution images for information only, reproduced under fair use terms. It is believed that these images will not devalue the ability of the copyright holder to profit from the original work. – *Marcus Welby MD.* cast, source: commons.wikimedia.org/wiki/File:Marcus_Welby_MD_cast.JPG. Pre 1978, no copyright mark (PD image).
Page 42– Sonny & Cher publicity image by CBS Television, 1971. Source: en.wikipedia.org/wiki/Sonny_%26_Cher#/media/File:Sonny_and_Cher_1971.JPG. (PD image). – *The New Dick Van Dyke Show*, by CBS. This is a low-resolution image for information only, reproduced under fair use terms. It is believed that this image will not devalue the ability of the copyright holder to profit from the original work. – *Columbo*, publicity photo by NBC, 31st May 1973. Source: commons. wikimedia.org/wiki/Category:People_of_the_United_States_in_1973#/media/File: Columbo_Peter_Falk_1973.JPG. (PD image*). – *The Two Ronnies*, image from the 1971-1987 TV series(complete series) DVD-R. Pre 1978 (PD image).
Page 43 – From *Life* Magazine 8th Jan 1971: books.google.com/books?id=nFMEAAAAMBAJ&printsec. (PD* image).

Page 44 – Walt Disney World images, sources: disneyparks.disney.go.com/blog/2010/10/this-day-in-history-walt-disney-world-resort-officially-opens-1971/, flickr.com/photos/iainstars/19490317806/ and en.wikipedia.org/wiki/Walt_Disney_World. All images Attribution-ShareAlike 4.0 International (CC BY-SA 4.0)

Page 45 – Webber, 2006. Source: commons.wikimedia.org/wiki/Category:Andrew_Lloyd_Webber (PD image). – Production photos from *Jesus Christ Superstar* (1971) by Friedman-Abeles, from New York Public Library Billy Rose Theatre Division. Shelf locator: *T-VIM 1992-013. Source: digitalcollections.nypl.org/items/c6adebf8-212c-4780-e040-e00a1806321a. Images, where not in the public domain, are reproduced here under terms of fair use. These are low-resolution images for information only, it is believed these will not prevent the copyright holder's ability to profit from the original works.

Page 46 – Still images from the films *Needle Park* by 20th Century Fox and *Carnal Knowledge* by AVCO Embassy Pictures. Reproductions included here for information only under U.S. fair use laws due to: 1- No free alternative can exist of trademarked characters; 2- images are low resolution copies and are too small for reproduction; 3- images do not limit the copyright owner's rights to profit from the works; 4- The images are significant to the article created.

Page 47 & 48 – Film posters for the movies *A Clockwork Orange* by Warner Bros. , *Fiddler on the Roof* by United Artists, and *The French Connection* by 20th Century Fox. – *The Poseidon Adventure* by 20th Century Fox, *The Towering Inferno* by 20th Century Fox, *Earthquake* by Universal Pictures, and *Tidalwave* by Toho. These are low-resolution images reproduced under fair use terms. It is believed these will not devalue the ability of the copyright holders to profit from their works.

Page 50 – Marvin Gaye album cover by Tamla (Motown Records) and John Lennon *Imagine* album cover by Apple Records. Images are reproduced under fair use terms for informational purposes only. No alternative free image exists. These images are of low resolution and will not devalue the ability of the creator to profit from the original works.

Page 51 – Glastonbury pyramid stage by Robert Bloomfield, 1971. Source: metro.co.uk/2011/06/ 23/glastonbury-festival-1971-a-blast-from-the-glast-55527/?ito=cbshare. – Celebration of Life, creator unknown. Source: stereolp.blogspot.com/2010/06/celebration-of-life-festival-june-21-28.html. Pre 1978, no copyright mark (PD* image).

Page 52 – Rod Stuart (cropped photo) for Mercury Records in *Billboard* 6th Nov 1971. Source: commons.wikimedia.org/wiki/Category:Rod_Stewart. Pre 1978, no copyright mark (PD image). – The Osmonds publicity photo for MGM Records, 28th Nov 1971. Source: commons.wikimedia.org/wiki/Category:The_Osmonds (PD image). – John Denver publicity photo for RCA records, 9th Aug 1973. Source: commons.wikimedia.org/wiki/Category:John_Denver. Pre 1978, no copyright mark (PD image). – The Bee Gees on *The Midnight Special*, NBC TV, 1973 Source: commons.wikimedia.org/wiki/Category:Bee_Gees. Pre 1978, no copyright mark (PD image).

Page 53 – Tom Jones, from ABC Television *This is Tom Jones*, 10th Nov 1969. Permission PD-PRE1978. Source: commons.wikimedia.org/wiki/Category:Tom_Jones_(singer). Pre 1978, (PD image). – The Carpenters, White House photo by Knudsen, Robert L from the National Archives, Identifier (NAID) 194770. (PD image).

Page 54 – Source: flickr.com/photos/nesster/5749980453/ by Nesster. Attribution 4.0 International (CC BY 4.0).

Page 55 – Advertisement from *Life* Magazine 4th June 1971. Source: books.google.com/books?id=Q0EEAAAAMBAJ&printsec. Pre 1978, no copyright mark (PD* image).

Page 56 – Pants and skirt-suit, 1969, creator unknown. Pre 1978, (PD image).– Maxi-dress by YSL, Spring-Summer 1969. Source: minniemuse.com/articles/creative-connections/ patchwork. Pre 1978, (PD image).

Page 57 – Elizabeth Taylor, source: instyle.com/celebrity/transformations/elizabeth-taylors-changing-looks. – Caftan dress, photographer unknown. Source: pinterest.com/pin/214624738475851800/. Pre 1978 (PD image). – Balestra dress from Italia Vogue, Feb 1970, photo by Barry Lategan. Pre 1978, (PD image). – Mini dresses, sources: pinterest.com/pin/9978294796766997/ and retrospace.org/2011_01_01_archive.html unknown photographers. Pre 1978, (PD image).

Page 58 – Fashions from Sears Catalogues, pre 1978, no copyright mark (PD image). – Hungarian singer Szűcs Judit wears embroidered demin. Source: commons.wikimedia.org/wiki/File:Szűcs_Judit_énekesnő._Fortepan_88657.jpg. Licensed under the Creative Commons Attribution-Share Alike 3.0 Unported. – Dacron pants from the 1975 J.C. Penney catalog. Pre 1978, (PD image). – Flared jumpsuits, creator unknown. Pre 1978, (PD image).

Page 59 – Advertisement from *Life* Magazine 7th May 1971. Source: books.google.com/books?id=LUAEAAAAMBAJ&printsec. Pre 1978, no copyright mark (PD* image).

Page 60 – Nik Nik shirts, polyester jumpsuits, and knit pantsuits, source: onedio.com/haber/erkekte-retro-modasinin-tutmamasinin-32-mantikli-sebebi-300983. – Polyester tops and pants, toweling jumpsuits, and shrink tops by Colombia Minerva, source: flashbak.com/the-good-the-bad-and-the-tacky-20-fashion-trends-of-the-1970s-26213/. – Denim on denim source: typesofjeanfits.com/a-brief-history-of-jeans-denim-history-timeline/. – Safari suits source: klyker.com/1970s-fashion/. All images this page pre 1978, no copyright mark or renewal (PD image).

Page 61 – Still image from the film *Saturday Night Fever* by Paramount Pictures. Source: vocal.media/beat/the-list-saturday-night-fever-40th-anniversary. This is a low-resolution image for information only, reproduced under fair use terms. It is believed this image will not devalue the ability of the copyright holders to profit from the original works. – Dancers Studio 54, sources: definition.org/studio-54/2/ & alexilubomirski.com/image-collections/studio-54 (PD images).

Page 62 – From *Life* Magazine 3rd Dec 1971. Source: books.google.com/books?id=HUAEAAAAMBAJ&printsec. (PD* image).

Page 63 – Ali vs Frazier, promotional poster. Source: en.wikipedia.org/wiki/Joe_Frazier#/media/File:Ali_vs_frazier_elgra fico.jpg. Pre 1978 (PD images). – Kahn, creator unknown. Source: dawn.com/news/1423231. Pre 1978, no copyright mark (PD images). – Goolagong, 1st Aug 1971, from Nationaal Archief. Source: nationaalarchief.nl/onderzoeken/fotocollectie/abc86f8c-d0b4-102d-bcf8-003048976d84. Pre 1978 (PD images). – King in 1973, unknown creator. Source: en.wikipedia.org/wiki/Billie_Jean_King#/media/File:Billie_Jean_King_and_Bobby_Riggs_1973.jpg. Pre 1978 (PD images).

Page 64 – From *Life* Magazine 7th May 1971. Source: books.google.com/books?id=LUAEAAAAMBAJ&printsec. (PD* image).

Page 65 – Computers at BBN Technologies, source: en.wikipedia.org/wiki/History_of_email#/media/File:Timesharing_and_Development_KA-10s_at_BBN,_circa_1970.jpg (PD image). – Tomlinson, source: en.wikipedia.org/wiki/Ray_Tomlinson#/media/File:Ray_Tomlinson_(cropped).jpg. Attribution-ShareAlike 3.0 Unported (CC BY-SA 3.0).

Page 66 – San Fernando collapsed highway by Reuben Kachadoorian, USGS, for the US Dept of the Interior. Source: commons.wikimedia.org/wiki/File:1971_San_Fernando_highway_overpass_collapse.jpg. Govt photo (PD image). – Mt Etna, creator unknown. Source: italysvolcanoes.com/gifs/image/1971StuBW_01.jpg. Pre 1978, (PD image). – Golden Gate Bridge by Matt Faluotico. Source: commons.wikimedia.org/wiki/Category:Golden_Gate_Bridge#/media/File:Almost_Baker_Beach_(135919049).jpeg licensed under Creative Commons Attribution 3.0 Unported.

Page 67 – Kennedy Center, unknown photographer. Source: commons.wikimedia.org/wiki/File:KennedyCenterFromAir2. JPG (PD image). – Neruda by Annemarie Heinrich, 1967. Source: commons.wikimedia.org/wiki/Category:Portraits_of_Pablo_Neruda#/media/File:Pablo_Neruda_by_Annemarie_Heinrich,_1967.jpg. (PD image).

Page 68 & 69 – All photos are, where possible, CC BY 2.0 or PD images made available by the creator for free use including commercial use. Where commercial use photos are unavailable, photos are included here for information only under U.S. fair use laws due to: 1- images are low resolution copies; 2- images do not devalue the ability of the copyright holders to profit from the original works in any way; 3- Images are too small to be used to make illegal copies for use in another book; 4- The images are relevant to the article created.

Page 70 – Advertisement from *Life* Magazine 2nd July 1971. Source: books.google.com/books?id=OUAEAAAAMBAJ&printsec. Pre 1978, no copyright mark (PD* image).

*Advertisement (or image from an advertisement) is in the public domain because it was published in a collective work (such as a periodical issue) in the US between 1925 and 1977 and without a copyright notice specific to the advertisement.

These words first appeared in print in the year 1971.

Passive smoking

sell-by date

beatbox

Loony Tunes

animatronics

CHEAP SHOT

username

automatic teller

WILD CARD

Asperger's Syndrome

knackered

MINIBAR

blow-dryer

sexual assault

cross-sell

KICKBOXING

reboot

*From merriam-webster.com/time-traveler/1971.

Please help me out:

I sincerely hope you enjoyed reading this book and that it brought back many fond memories from the past.

I have enjoyed researching and writing this book for you and would greatly appreciate your feedback by way of a written review and/or star rating.

First and foremost, I am always looking to grow and improve as a writer. It is reassuring to hear what works, as well as to receive constructive feedback on what could improve.

Second, starting out as an unknown author is exceedingly difficult, and Customer Reviews go a long way toward making the journey out of anonymity possible.

Please help me by taking a few moments to leave a review for others to read.

Best regards,
Bernard Bradforsand-Tyler.

Please leave a
book review/rating at:

http://bit.ly/1971reviews

Or scan the QR code:

Made in the USA
Monee, IL
04 September 2021